YOUR KNOWLEDGE HAS VALUE

Yelyzaveta Babenko

Analysis of the film "The Matrix"

GRIN Publishing

Bibliographic information published by the German National Library:

The German National Library lists this publication in the National Bibliography; detailed bibliographic data are available on the Internet at http://dnb.dnb.de .

Imprint:

Copyright © 2010 GRIN Verlag, Open Publishing GmbH
Print and binding: Books on Demand GmbH, Norderstedt Germany
ISBN: 978-3-640-91285-8

This book at GRIN:

http://www.grin.com/en/e-book/171805/analysis-of-the-film-the-matrix

GRIN - Your knowledge has value

Since its foundation in 1998, GRIN has specialized in publishing academic texts by students, college teachers and other academics as e-book and printed book. The website www.grin.com is an ideal platform for presenting term papers, final papers, scientific essays, dissertations and specialist books.

Visit us on the internet:

http://www.grin.com/

http://www.facebook.com/grincom

http://www.twitter.com/grin_com

Contents

1. Introduction

Is is only in the last decades of the twentieth century that technology gained an important place in western society, and its development is flourishing up to the present day.

Due to the rapid progress of high-tech computers and information technology the standard of living improved, and full scope can be given to our creativity, for mechanical tasks are now fulfiled by the machines.

The Technological Revolution has aroused several expectations and fantasies. The seemingly utopistic idea of artificial intelligence which has moved human beings since the antiquity appeared by the midth of the twentieth century more than ever realistic.

Such a promising future vision has otherwise led to anxiety and fear. What if we will, striving after power, lose it completely and get ourselves into bondage?

These thoughts gave birth to anti-utopian fiction where the worst of the fears are brought into reality – intelligent machines created by human beings have made people to their slaves and rule on Earth.

2. The Matrix

2. 2 About the film[1]

An example for such a vision is "The Matrix", an American science-fiction-action film written and directed by Larry and Andy Wachowski starring Keanu Reeves, Laurence Fishburne, Carrie-Anne Moss and Hugo Weaving. It was released in March 1999 and has won four Oscars. Two sequels, "The Matrix Reloaded" and "The Matrix Revolutions" were released in 2003.

2. 3. Prehistory [2]

At the beginning of the twenty first century people create intelligent robots and machines to exploit them as simple workers. Though working hard and tirelessly these ones are treated disrespectfully, until one day machine B1-66ER stands up to his master and murders him. After that riots break out, and the machines protest for a better treatment. The human beings act with extreme violence even against peacefully demonstrating roboters, a machine genocide starts.

The escaped machines form a new nation they call "01" (Zero One), where technological development rapidly proceeds so that 01 soon occupies a leading economic position. Many nations boycott Zero One afraid of the power Zero One could gain and refuse their accession to the United Nations Organisation.

Five years after this inccident, in the year 2094, the humans commence a war against the machines which, having survived the bombing, counter-attack the human beings.

Inferior to the robots, the people decide to destroy the sun, the main source of energy for the machines.

The war ends in 2139 with the victory of the robots who kill the leaders of the human army with a nuclear bomb, the rebellion breaks up, people flee to Zion, a city in the Earth's interior.

All people except the escaped ones are prisoners of the machines which exploit them as "living batteries" and imprison their minds within an artificial reality known as "The Matrix".

This is the prehistory of the film which is partly revealed in "The Matrix" and explained more detailed in "Animatrix", a collection of seven animated short films about the conflict between machines and humans.

A group of humans can free their minds and release themselves from the simulated reality being subsequently able to unplug their physical bodies from the mechanical tower the "human batteries" are connected to. They live in ships located underground in former canalisation.

The story of "The Matrix" itself takes place in estimated 2199, the rebels themselves do not exactly know the date[3].

There are some few ships and one of them is called Nebukadnezzar.

The leader of the rebellion on this ship and its commander, Morpheus, believes to have found the "saviour" who according to the prophecy will one day arrive and release the humans from the despoty of the machines.

The supposed saviour is a computer programmer Thomas A. Anderson who leads a secret life as a hacker under the alias "Neo".

The underground hacker Morpheus stamped in the matrix as a dangerous terrorist intrigues Neo who is already for a long time searching for the truth.

2. 4. Plot Summary

"The Matrix" shows the transformation of a regular human being Thomas A. Anderson to the saviour Neo able to bend and break the rules of the computer generated reality, the Matrix, and his fight against the machines[4].

2. 5. Analysis

2.5.1. System Functionality

The Matrix is the main computer which puts the Matrix of life, the simulated reality, in the individual computer, the human brain.

Perceptual consciousness contained in every individual computer provides the energy of life. (*See Figure 1*)

2.5.2. The Title[5]

The title of the film has several meanings and definitions. Some of them will be presented in the following.

In Mathematics a matrix is "a rectangular array of elements set out in rows and columns, used to facilitate the solution of problems, such as the transformation of coordinates."

Furthermore, the word "matrix" means "a substance, situation, or environment in which something has its origin, takes form, or is enclosed."

Active matrix is moreover a "technology used in the flat and liquid crystal displays of notebooks and laptop computers."

In cyberspace, the internet and other networks that flow into it are sometimes called "the matrix."

In William Gibson's science-fiction novel "Neuromancer" the "matrix" refers to computing resources that can be visualised holographically by the user.

In the film the Matrix is, on the one hand, a holographic reality but it also refers to the secret cypher which is called "matrix".

On the other hand, human beings are born in the Matrix, so is "an environment where something has its origin".

2.5.3. Number Symbolism[6]

Room number 101

The first number shown in „The Matrix" is the number of Neo's room – 101. There are various interpretations of the symbolic value of this number.

4

The number 101 consists of two digits – one and zero.

Taking the Pythagorean doctrines of number into consideration[7], a distinction between odd and even numbers should be made. According to the Pythagoreans, odd numbers are perfect since they are not divisible into equal parts without remainder. The number one is an odd number and therefore a symbol for unity, it is the number of reason, the generator of numbers. The number zero has an oval form, it is so to say a closed ring and stands therefore for endlessness which means perfection on the one hand and a vicious circle, a situation without any outcome, a perpetual recursion of actions on the other hand. Endlessness has no limits, and the one who dares to enter the endlessness risks to stir towards a distraction.

This number can also symbolise freedom, because freedom is closely linked with infinity. Zero recalls associations with an embryo in the womb and can symbolise the regeneration circle, the transition from one life to another.

Besides, a further word for "womb" is "matrix"[8].

When interpreting the symbolism of "zero" from this point of view, the "matrix" is the number one which is perfect and though static and rigid. Neo can be compared to an embryo caught in this "matrix", blind and unaware.

A further hypothesis can be made if we take the number 101 as a whole into consideration. Thus 101 is nothing but an element of a program, an element of the binary system used internally by all modern computers. It is rigid computer logic detecting nothing but the conditions signal/ no signal.

According to that, Neo, whom the room 101 belongs to, lives within a computer program, he is caught in this simulation amenable to binary computer logic.

Furthemore, "Neo" is the anagramm of "One", thus the number 101 can represent Neo himself.

In George Orwell's book "1984", a famous anti-utopian novel, the "mysterious room 101" is the place where people are tortured and forced to believe in lies coming out with imprisoned minds.

As we know, Neo's mind during his presence in the room 101 is not free, as well. He believes in a simulation, controled by the machines.

Room number 303

The second remarkable number is the hotel room number 303 appearing twice.

At the beginning of the film Trinity observes Neo from a computer in the hotel "Heart O' the City" in room number 303. The song playing in the background is titled "Main theme/Trinity infinity".

According to that, the number 303 may represent Trinity herself, for the number "3" stands for trinity, the number "0" is a circle and therefore represents infinity. In Christian theology there are three entities forming a single God: Father, Son and Holy Spirit, this is the trinity of God. [9]

Additionally, it is in the same location that Neo is killed by agent Smith and is finally ressurected.

The moment of Neo's death is the apogee of the bondage of his mind – Neo dies in the Matrix because his "mind makes it real" as Morpheus says to him during his training. At that moment tha machines can yet control Neo and have the power of him.

But then Trinity, who is in the real world, talks to Neo and forces Neo's mind, his beliefs, the rationalism, to gain power over the empirical knowledge, and Neo ressurects.

The cube of "101" when taking the digits separately amounts in "303" which would support the idea of the apogee of Neo's belief in illusion. So the number 303 may represent both Trinity herself and Neo's release of chains imprisonning his mind. Besides, it is in both cases Trinity who appears, mentally or physically, in this room.

2.5.4. Names in „The Matrix"

Choi and Dujour

The first people Neo encounters in the film are Choi and his girlfriend Dujour, probably an allusion on the french phrase „Choix du jour" which means "Choice of the day". Neo makes the crucial choice going with them to the club, following the "white rabbit".

Morpheus[10]

In Greek mythology, Morpheus is the God of dreams. In the film he is the resistance leader who awakens people from the "dream" , as their existance in the Matrix can be described. For Morpheus knows that this existence is a simulation, a dream, he has the power of it, "For knowledge is power" (F. Bacon).

Morpheus' hovercraft is called Nebudadnezzar. In the bible, Nebukadnezzar II was a Babylonian king and de facto the founder of later Babylon. He searched for the meaning of his dreams and ordered to call in the Chaldeans, the magicians and other wisemen. As nobody of them new the answer, Nebukadnezzar ordered to kill all the wisemen of Babylon. Thereafter God revealed the secret of Nebukadnezzar's dreams to a wiseman, and the latter interpreted the dreams for Nebukadnezzar.

In the film, Morpheus seeks advice from the Oracle. By the way, the correct spelling of "Nebukadnezzar" is "Nabu-ku-dur-ri-u-su-ur". Nabu is the Babylonian god of wisdom.

Thus, on the one hand, Morpheus represents wisdom, power and greatness.

Like all the other resistance leaders, Morpheus, the commander of Nebukadnezzar, knows the access codes to Zion's mainframe computer. Zion in "The Matrix" is the last human city that exists after the destruction of the earth.

In the "Book of Revelation", Zion is the holy city: "Kingdom of God in a New Heaven and New Earth" (21:5b-22:5) where the righteous will be saved after the destruction of the earth. Morpheus can therefore be understood as the saviour of the "the rigtheous", the members of his crew.

According to the Thesaurus, "morphing" means to "cause to change shape in a computer animation".

Stephen Kobourov and Matthew Landis write in their article "Morphing planar graphs in spherical space" for the "Journal of Graph Algorithms and Applications" that "Morphing refers to the process of transforming one shape (the source) into another (the target)".

It is due to Morpheus that Neo is transformed from Thomas Anderson into "The One", the saviour Neo.

The root word "morph" is also contained in "morphine". Morphine is an extremely addictive pain reliever. It furthermore induces sleep[11].

Taking this fact into consideration, the figure of Morpheus can either mean danger, since Morpheus is both able to awaken and to induce sleep or, what seems rather reasonable, the meaning is ironically twisted.

Whereas the narcotic morphine soothes pain and triggers sleep, Morpheus awakens people, and the reality they see is painful. Making a deal with agent Smith Cypher says "Ignorance is bliss" and betrays the rebels because he is not able to endure the reality. Not Morpheus is addictive but the simulated world the rebels lived in before he released them.

Trinity[12]

Trinity stands for the number three which the Pythagoreans believed to be perfect.

The number three is found on many pillars throughout the subway scene.

The word "trinity" is used to represent the union of three people; the connection of the body, mind and spirit; birth, life and death; or past, present and future.

In Christian theology, "trinity" refers to the trifold personality of a single God, the union of the Father, the Son (Christ), and the Holy Spirit.

In "The Matrix" Neo represents the Son, for he is claimed to be The One, the saviour. Neo's friend Choi calls Neo his "personal Jesus Christ". According to Tank's words, Morpheus is the Father for them all.

Trinity represents hence the Holy Spirit. This idea is supported by the fact that Neo hears and realises Trinity's voice after his death, when she speaks to his physical body.

Neo/Thomas[13]

An anagram of Neo is One. According to the Wachowski brothers, "Neo is Thomas Anderson's potential self."

The name "Thomas" is Hebrew and means "twin". Neo lives two lives – the ordinary life of a computer programmer and the secret life of a hacker. The word "Neo" is Latin and means "New". It supports the role of Neo as the saviour – to defeat the machines and to change the world, bringing in a new order.

Thomas' last name is "Anderson", deriving from "Son of Andrew". This name is Greek and means "Man" . Thomas surname means thus "Man's Son" also referring to the Biblical Messiah.

Furthermore, Thomas appears in the Bible as the "Doubting Thomas", one of the Disciples of Jesus.

According to the Bible, he did not believe in the death and resurrection of Jesus until he saw the holes in his hands. Analogous to that, Thomas alias Neo does not realise that he is shut until he sees the bullet holes in his chest.

According to the principle of trinity, Neo represents the Son, as already discussed above.

The Oracle

In Christian Theology, the Delphic Oracle foretold the coming of the Messiah. In "The Matrix" the Oracle told Morpheus he would find The One.

Cypher[14]

Cypher is another form of the word, "Cipher." According to the American Heritage Dictionary "cipher" means "to be empty". Furthermore, it stands for "zero" in the arithmetical system. It is thus something of no value or importance, a non-entity. Therefore, Cypher is a person of no influence and this is one of the reasons for his betrayal. Cypher prefers to be someone in the Matrix instead of being a "zero" in the reality.
Cypher also means a secret code, which corresponds with the code of the matrix in the film.

Apoc[15]

It is an abbreviation for "Apocalypse" which means, according the American Heritage Dictionary, "A prophetic disclosure; a revelation" or "an event of great importance". This defintions correspond with the arrival of The One which was prophecised by the Oracle.

Tank and Dozer[16]

A tank and a bulldozer are mechanical machines that make a lot of noise. In "The Matrix" the two brothers are followers of Morpheus. This exhibits parallels to the Apostles of Christ, brothers James and John who are referred to in the Bible as "sons of thunder".

2.5.5. Philosophy in "The Matrix"

"Have you ever had a dream, Neo, that you were so sure was
real? What if you were unable to wake from that dream? How
would you know the difference, between the dream world...and
the real world....?" [17]

This is the question Morpheus asks Neo before unplugging him from the Matrix and
returning Neo to the "real world", to *their* real world.

For it is a deeply philosophical question – what the real world actually is, and the answers can
differ entirely.

The rationalist Descartes[18] argued that the senses deceive us, and the only method that could
be applied to find out the truth is according to Descartes that of the doubt. He stated that as
long as I am doubting, I can assume that my "I" exists. Thus the truth can only be found out
through the common sense, the *ratio (lat.)*.

One of the most important representatives of British Empiricism, David Hume, rejected this
theory and stated that the reality can be constructed of the succession of individual
experiences[19].

At first sight the Matrix appears for Neo as the real world than Morpheus reveals to him the
truth about the simulated reality Neo lives in. Morpheus is the rationalist accepting nothing
but the common sense: "Your mind makes it real...", - says Morpheus to astonished Neo who
has just fallen down from a skyscraper in the matrix and wonders why does he have blood in
the mouth. Neo's common sense has persuaded Neo of the happening as a fact. Due to
Morpheus Neo learns to break the rules of the Matrix. He succeeds after being entirely
convinced of the fact that the Matrix is not real. And though he does gain experience in the
Matrix, and due to this succession of personal experiences Neo's personality is formed and
developed. The less does Neo believe in the reality of the Matrix, the more real is the
experience he gains within it. Would not it support the Empiricist Hume?

According to Immanuel Kant, the truth corresponds with the human mind in a certain way and
is not universally valid. Kant's concept of the truth has though transcendent traits.

Neo's truth is definitely not generally valid and certainly transcends the empirical knowledge.
In "Matrix Reloaded" Neo encounters the Architect, the Demiurg of the programm who
reveals to Neo that he is not The One. He is only one of many saviours and everything is
preprogrammed. Neo is a cyclic anomaly having come into existence because of a system
failure, but the Architect has everything under control.

Thus, in the second sequel of the Matrix Trilogy we get to know that the reality, the "truth" Morpheus and the other rebels are fighting for is nothing but a utopia, an imagination, an illusion.

At the beginning of the film Neo takes a cederom for Choi from the book "Simulacra and Simulation". It is a philosophical treatise by Jean Baudrillard.

Baudrillard argues that the modern society has replaced all reality with symbols and signs[20]. Therefore, the human beings experience the simulation of reality not the reality itself. The simulacra are signs of culture and media, based on the reality, which create the perceived reality.

Perhaps, it was the aim of the Wachowski brothers to make an allusion on the fact, that the reality we perceive is simulated, already at the beginning of their film. Jean Baudrillard himself states though that the Wachowski brothers misunderstand him. That is what he says in an interview for "Le nouvel Observateur" published in 2004:

"These people take the hypothesis of the virtual as a fact and carry it over to visible fantasms. But the primary characteristic of this universe lies precisely in the inability to use categories of the real to speak about it .[…] Anyway, the real nuisance in this movie is that the brand-new problem of the simulation is mistaken with the very classic problem of the illusion, already mentionned by Plato. Here lies the mistake."

However, the message the directors of "The Matrix" probably intended to convey, is correctly transmitted, for the majority of the people understand the theory of Jean Baudrillard just as the Wachowski Brothers do.

3. How realistic is the vision of the Matrix?

Entirely in accordance with the features of a dystopia "The Matrix" shows an imaginary distorted world in the era of Artificial Intelligence where human beings are imprisoned and exploited by the machines[21].

The crucial question is now, how close does this vision approach to reality.

In order to give a response to this question, the current state of computer science and psychological and philosophical investigations in relation to the field of Artificial Intelligence should be regarded more closely.

3. 1. History of Computer Science[22]

Many engineers, mathematicians and scientists have contributed to the development of the digital computer. The first computer was developed in 1642 by Blaise Pascale, and it was improved in 1670 by Gottfried Leibniz.

In the nineteenth century a mathematician called George Boole improved binary mathematics which contributed much to the development of computers. Further improvements and inventions were made during two previous centuries, one of the most significant inventions was the ENIAC (Electronic Numerical Integrator And Computer) developed in 1946. This computer weighted more than 27 metric tons, occupied more then 140 square metres of floor space and used 150 kilowatts of power during operation. It was able to do 5000 addition and 1000 multiplications per second.

Today, computers require more than 1000 times less energy, and the smallest computer in the world is not bigger than a mobile phone. Computers are now even integrated in mobile phones like I-Phone. Therefore, computer science is making rapid strides and, regarded from this perspective, the prospects on creating once an intelligent computer are in deed great.

3. 2. History of Artificial Intelligence[23]

The Foundations

First the idea of artificial intelligence appears in Greek mythology. For instance, in the classical myth of Pygmalion the protagonist carved a woman out of a tree. The statue called Galathea looked very realistic, and Pigmalion fell in love with her. He begged Aphrodite to bring the statue to life and the goddess fulfilled his wish.

In the fourth century B.C. the first system of formal reasoning, the syllogistic logic, was developed by Aristotle[24].

Of great importance is a method designed by Ramon Llull, a medieval philosopher, which was published in his "Ars Magna" in the thirteenth century. Through this method different attributes selected from a number of lists could be combined with each other. IT should be used as means to convert Muslims to the Christian faith through logic and reason. Llull's machine, called Lullian Circle, "allowed a reader to enter an argument or question about the Christian faith, and the reader would then turn to the appropriate index and page to find the correct answer."[25]

Pioneer contributions were also made by the French rationalist René Descartes who rejected the senses, because they can deceive. He proves it with the "dream argument" – during a dream the individual can be concerned of not dreaming for it appears to be real while the dream exists nowhere but in a subject's mind. Therefore, Descartes accepted nothing but the ratio (lat.), the common sense, as the highest authority.

Descartes implemented the method of scepsis according to which the individual has to question everything except of the fact, that it is doubting at the very moment of the act of the doubt. Descartes expresses that in the famous sentence "Cogito ergo sum"(lat.) meaning "I think, therefore I am".

René Descartes was a dualist and distinguished between mental substance and bodily substance. The mind-body distinction is very relevant in Artificial Intelligence. The human mind may be considered to be a piece of software which the human brain implements. Therefore, it should be possible to code this program on a von Neumann computer creating a mental machine.

One well-known argument against Cartesianism is the "brain in the vat" argument.

This is a thought experiment in which a mad scientist separates a brain of a subject from its body, puts the brain in a vat and connects it to a computer. Therefore, the person would think and doubt and could assume, according to Descartes, its existence during the act of thinking.

But the person would be mistaken for the brain is removed from the body and receives false perception.

Thus, it is impossible to tell whether the brain is inside the body or inside the vat. According to that you can't tell whether your belief is valid or not.

Just the same illusion believe the human beings in "The Matrix" whose bodies are in a "vat" and whose minds are within a computer program.

Descartes believed that the bodies of animals are machines without feelings, and he did many experiments on them.

Due to that he realised that some aspects in the human behaviour have a mechanistic explanation, like, for instance, physiological functions and blinking. Therefore, Descartes envisioned that well-designed mechanisms could mimic some features of the human behaviour.

Descartes stated that the crucial difference between animals and humans is, that human beings are able to act in several spheres, whereas animals concentrate on a certain limited sphere where they can develop their instincts wholly. Language derives thus from the lack of instinct. This distinction provides evidence for the fact that humans are, unlike the animals, machines with soul and not simply pure machines.

The significance of Descartes in the field of Artificial Intelligence is that the Cartesian dualism that humans seem to possess would need to be reflected among artificial machines. The "I" of the humans represents personhood for it is independent from their body.Therefore, the challenge for the developers of AI would be to create such a machine that posesses this distinction between body and mind.

In the seventienth century Thomas Hobbes published "Leviathan". In this work he wrote "...for reason is nothing but reckoning" presenting thus a new, mechanical theory of cognition.

Important inventions in computer science were made by Gottfried von Leibniz and Blaise Pascale[26]. Leibniz furthermore had the idea of a universal calculus of reasoning by which arguments could be decided mechanically.

In 1727 Jonathan Swift published "Gulliver's Travels" where "Ars Magna" is parodied through the figure of the engine on the island of Laputa.

In 1818 Mary Shelley's "Frankenstein" was published, a story of an artificially created sentient being.

Further important scientific inventions were made by Charles Babbage, George Boole, Konrad Zuse and John von Neumann contributing to the development and transformation of the idea of AI[27].

In 1950 Alan Turing, a British mathematician, developed the Turing Test according to which it should be possible to decide whether a machine is conscious and intelligent. This invention raised the idea of programming a computer to behave intelligent.

Turing statement that it is possible to construct such a machine which, given a right programm,. would have mental properties of a human, is known as "strong artificial intelligence".

In the same year Claude Shannon published an article considering the possibility of writing a chess programm. Such a programm would be able to play chess, and this is intelligent, but the programm itself would not be conscious that it is playing chess.

The term Artificial Intelligence is first used as the topic of the Second Dartmouth Conference organised by John McCarthy, an American computer scientist and cognitive scientist, in 1956. He was the first to propose to employ logic as the method to represent information in computer memory. Namely, such a computer programm would use syllogistic logic, that is to make conclusions from a set of premises. So, expressed by O'Reagan "the program manipulates the formal language (e.g., predicate logic), and provides a conclusion that may be a statement or an imperative".

McCarthy argues that a programm has common sense if it is able to automatically deduce conslusions from the previous knowledge and the premises given.

In conclusion, McCarthy's thesis was that common sense problems can be solved by logical reasonning for common sense knowledge is formalised by logic.

Philosophy and Artificial Intelligence

The French Rationalism represented by René Descartes and its contributions to the field of Artificial Intelligence were already discussed beyond[28].

The Cartesianism rejects all senses and argues that all knowledge is derived from the common sense. In opposition to this theory, the British Empiricism states that all knowledge can be gained through sense experience. The represantatives of this theory were Hobbes, Locke, Berkeley and Hume.

The latter made a clear distinction between ideas and impressions. According to Hume, "impression" is the perception of direct experience through the senses of hearing, seeing and so on. Ideas are the reflections on sensations. Therefore, every idea must be a copy from the impressions. According to Hume, there are three relations between impressions and ideas: ressemblance, spacio-temporal contiguity and effect.

Hume distinguished between two kinds human knowledge: "relations of ideas", that can be verified logically for they only exist in our mind, and "matter of fact". The evidence for the truth of this kind of knowledge is based o experience.

A response to Hume's theory is given by Immanuel Kant in his "Critique of Pure Reason"[29] published in 1781. Kant defines a third kind of knowledge that can't derive from experience. This third force structures the experience and includes entities such as modus ponens[30].

In the early twentieth century the analytic school of philosophy came up.

This school believed that many philosophical problems remain unsolved due to the lack of scientific knowledge.

According to this theory some questions of cognition and its limits could be answered due to scientific progress. This position supports the idea of consctucting Artificial Intelligence for it is, in principle, possible to explore the human's mind and to imitate it artificially.

Cognitive Psychology[31] and Artificial Intelligence

Cognitive psychology is a discipline, developed in 1950s, that investigates the mental processes such as visual processing that take place during a stimulus and the reaction on it. Cognitive psychology views cognition as the processing of sensory input. The information processing model is an important concept in this field. This model supposes that the mental processes in a human mind are equivalent to the software running on the computer. Cognitive psychology has been studied in connection with artificial intelligence from the 1960s.

Investigations are conducted in the areas perception, memory, language, thinking, knowle representation and others. This research is very important for the developments in Artificial Intelligence, for an intelligent machine must be able to perceive empirical data, to process it and to remember knowledge. Furthermore, such a machine must be able to understand and apply both written language and language in audio form.

4. Conclusion

Although pioneer inventions have been made in the field of computer science, and digital computers, based on binary logic, integrally gained in importance, despite many crucial discoveries in the field of cognitive psychology, due to which many processes in the human mind can be today logically explained, the field of Artificial Intelligence remains only partly explored.

The construction of a thinking machine that is intelligent, has consciousness, has free will, is ethical and is able to learn yet remains an imaginary idea, a utopia – or a dystopia, it depends on the perspective.

---

[1] [IS:59]; Internet Source.
[2] [FS:02]; Film Source.
[3] [FS:01]
[4] [Bab:10.3]

[5] [AHD:00]; [THE:06]
[6] [IS:36;40;41]
[7] [IS:41]
[8] [AHD:00]
[9] [Hem:95]
[10] [IS:55;59]
[11] [IS:55]
[12] [Hem:95]
[13] [NAB:95]
[14] [IS:52]
[15] [AHD:00];[THE:06]
[16] [AHD:00];[THE:06]
[17] [Bab:10.3; ll. 29-31]
[18] [Des:99]
[19] [ORg:08]
[20] [Bau:94]
[21] [AHD:00];[THE:06]
[22] [Bab:10.1]
[23] [ORg:08] *for further information see [Bab:10.2]
[24] [Bab:10.1]
[25] [ORg:08]
[26] [Bab:10.1]
[27] [Bab:10.1]
[28] see: History of Artificial Intelligence. The Foundations
[29] [Kan:03]
[30] [IS:48]
[31] [IS:47;50]

Attachment

History of Computer Science

A foundation for computer science

The history of computing goes back at least 3,000 years ago. Early civilizations like the Babylonians, Greeks, Egyptians, Indians, Chinese put the foundation for modern computer science.

The first important development is the abacus, the first known calculator (see table).

The Antikythera is considered to be the first mechanical analogue computer (see table). Arithmetic computation was automatised and simplificated during the first half of the 17th century. In 1621 William Oughtred developed the first slide rule, just after the concept of the logarithm was published by John Napier. A slide rule is a hand-operated analogue computer able to do multiplication and division.

In 1642 Blaise Pascal developed a machine with cogs and gears which is claimed to be the first digital computer.

In 1674 Gottfried von Leibnitz invented a mechanical calculator, the Leibnitz Wheel (see picture) for doing addition, subtraction, multiplication, and division. He created a special stepped cylindrical gear which is still being used.

But neither the machine of Pascal or the Leibnitz Wheel can be called computers because they did not have memory where information could be saved. Furthermore, they were not programmable. The Jacquard Loom, invented by Joseph Jacquard in 1801, did satisfy these requirements. Due to this invention the process of weaving was automated. The machine used punched cards telling her what pattern to weave.

Not much progress was made for the next centuries until the matematician George Boole invented the Boolean algebra (see table) in 1850s having put the basis for modern computers. In 1822 Charles Babbage had an idea of an automatic mechanical calculating machine which he called the "Difference Engine". IN 1833 Babbage made a new invention – a completely

19

program-controlled digital computer, the "Analytical Engine" which used <u>punched cards</u> and should be operated by only one person. Babbage's engines were never finished.

during the late 1800's a big immigration wave flow over America. The census was conducted manually and it would have taken over ten years to do this. The American Census Bureau held a competition searching for better solutions. The competition was won by Herman Hollerith who automated the process through creating programmable card proseccing machines. These machines were able to read and sort data from punched cards.

Babylon	c. 2400 BC	The abacus, the first known calculator, is invented by Babylonians
Egypt	c. 1832 BC	Rhind Papyrus; contains of various geometric and arithmetic problems
Greece	500-600 BC	Mathematicians Pythagoras and Thales
India	c. 500 BC	First known use of zero
India	c. 500 BC	Indian mathematician and linguist Panini formulated the grammar of Sanscrit
India	400 BC – 400 AD	Development of the decimal notation of numbers
China	400 BC	Invention of a counting board (an early version of abacus)
	c. 300 BC	Euclid, the father of geometry: axiomatic method for mathematics[1]
Greece	384 BC-322 BC	Development of syllogistic logic[2] and foundational work in modal logic (Aristotle)
India	c. 300 BC	The binary number system, on which all modern computing equipment is based, is invented by the Indian mathematician Pingala
Greece	300 BC	An early form of propositional logic[3] (Chrysippus)
Rome	290 BC	An early banking system is invented by Roman merchants. They commence minting money.
Greece	80 BC	Invention of the Antikythera[4] to calculate astronomical positions
Rome	100 BC-44 BC	Gaius Iulius Caesar, a Roman Imperator, invents the Caesar Cipher.
	c. 60 AD	The "Sequence Control" is invented by Heron of Alexandria which actually is the first program.

Ad 1

A method to derive and prove theorems setting out from 5 axioms, 5 postulates and 23 definitions.

Ad 2

This was a pioneering contribution to formal reasoning. Syllogistic logic consists of two premises and one conclusion. Each premise contains two terms. The first premise is a universal statement, and the second premise is a single clause. One term of the two premises is common in both of them. The two other terms are linked in the conclusion. Example:

Premise 1: All women are unreasonable.
Premise 2: Anna is a woman.
Conclusion: Anna is unreasonable.

Ad 3

Propositional logic is a formal system where the formulas have a certain truth value –a formula can be either true or false. Formulas which can be concluded from axioms and inference rules in the formal system are called theorems (true propositions). A succession of formulas in a formal system is called a derivation. The last formula in the succession is a theorem derived from previous formulas in the series.
Propositional logic or propositional calculus was developed by George Boole in the nineteenth century but remained relatively unknown until Glaude Shannon's investigations in the 1930s. Shannon demonstrated the usefulness of Boolean algebra to society employing the propositional calculus for switching telephone routes.

Ad 4

This mechanical device is based on the differential gear and considered to be the first analog computer.

Two types of computers

Digital computer

A digital computer is, according to Britannica Concise Encyclopedia, a computer that "accepts and processes data that has been converted into binary numbers".

The basic functional elements of a digital computer are input-output-equpment, main memory, control unit and arithmetic-logic unit (picture).

This concept was proposed in 1946 by John-Von-Neumann, an American matematician.

The control unit, which serves to extract and decode instructions from memory and the ALU, which performs all the arithmetic and logic operations, are in the central Processing Unit, the CPU.

CPU is the "brain" of any computer system because it makes all calculations and actuvates and controls the operations.

Apart from the control unit and the ALU, CPU has two further key parts – the temporary storage units (registers), the accumulator or the program counter for example, and the clock which generates electronic pulses to synchronise operations in the CPU.

The input devicec are for example keyboard, mouse and scanner. They serve to put the information in the computer.

The output devices are used to receive processed data from the computer. Monitor and printer are for instance output devices.

Analogue computer

An analogue computer is a device that, accrding to " the Computer Desktop Encyclopedia "processes infinitely varying signals such as electrical potential, hydraulics or mechanical motion, contrastive to the digital computer, which processes descrete data.

The original is simulated in an analogue model and the solution is given by measuring the variables. A thermometer is a simple analogue computer.

Birth of computers (1940-1950)

Two types of a computer

The most significant date in the history of computer technology is the year 1936. In this year Konrad Zuse created the first computer called Z1. It can be categorized as computer for it is completely programmable.

Many calculations had to be made during the Second World War. In 1931 the U.S. Navy and IBM (International Business Machines Corporation) created a general-purpose computer called the Mark 1 which was the first computer using binary system. But the disadvantage was that Mark 1 was absolutely gigantic.

Due to the need in artillery, a fully electronic computing device was designed in 1943 by J. Presper Eckert and John Mauchly, the Electronic Numerical Integrator and Calculator (ENIAC). Another computer was the Colossus created by Alan Turing. The Colossus cracked the German Enigma code helping the Americans to defeat the national socialists.

First Generation (1950 - 1957)

In 1945 John Von Neumann, an American matematician introduced a new concept of a stored-programm digital computer (see above), and in 1951 he implemented his idea in EDVAC.

Important engineering discoveries were made in the 1950s. These discoveries were the Transistor-Circuit Element and the magnetic core memory. The speed of data processing strikingly increased.

Second Generation (1957 - 1965)

In 1957 the first high-level programming language, the FORTRAN, was released for engineering and scientific use.

In 1959, the Common Business-Oriented Language (COBOL) was developed for business administration.

Third Generation (1965 - 1975)

In 1960 the Programmed Data Processor- 1 (PDP-1) was developed. It can be called the first mini-computer because of its small size.The PDP-1 was also the computer that ran the very first video game, called Spacewar (written in 1962).

The software industry came into existence in the 1970's as the number of computer users increased. E-mail originated between 1961 and 1966, allowing computer users who were connected through a network to send E-mails to each other.

Fourth Generation (1975 - 1985)

During this period computers had a size of a typewriter and were called minicomputers.

A small company called Apple Computer, Inc. was established in 1976. It's computer Apple1 came with a keyboard and only required a monitor to be plugged into the back of the system being a new idea to that time. Apple II lead to the era of personal computing.

In 1981, Microsoft Disk Operating System (MS-DOS) was released to run on the Intel 8086 microprocessor. IT became very popular and lead to Microsoft Windows 1.0 which was introduced in 1985.

In 1984 Apple introduced Mac OS, the first completely graphical operating system. The first mouse was developed in 1981 by Xerox.

The first truly portable computer, the Osborne 1, was released in 1981.

Furthermore, during this period embedded systems, systems with a computer inside to control their operation, were developed. They were put into cars, microwave ovens and more.

Fifth Generation (1985 - Present)

In the last decades of the twentieth century computers have become more and more integrated into the society, software is now included in automobiles, televisions and mobile phones. They gained even more popularity with the release of the World Wide Web in 1991.

The King's Forgotten Dream

1 Now in the second year of the reign of Nebuchadnezzar, Nebuchadnezzar had dreams; and his spirit was troubled and his sleep left him. 2 Then the king gave orders to call in the magicians, the conjurers, the sorcerers and the Chaldeans to tell the king his dreams. So they came in and stood before the king. 3 The king said to them, "I had a dream and my spirit is anxious to understand the dream."

4 Then the Chaldeans spoke to the king in Aramaic: "O king, live forever! Tell the dream to your servants, and we will declare the interpretation." 5 The king replied to the Chaldeans, "The command from me is firm: if you do not make known to me the dream and its interpretation, you will be torn limb from limb and your houses will be made a rubbish heap. 6 "But if you declare the dream and its interpretation, you will receive from me gifts and a reward and great honor; therefore declare to me the dream and its interpretation." 7 They answered a second time and said, "Let the king tell the dream to his servants, and we will declare the interpretation." 8 The king replied, "I know for certain that you are bargaining for time, inasmuch as you have seen that the command from me is firm, 9 that if you do not make the dream known to me, there is only one decree for you. For you have agreed together to speak lying and corrupt words before me until the situation is changed; therefore tell me the dream, that I may know that you can declare to me its interpretation." 10 The Chaldeans answered the king and said, "There is not a man on earth who could declare the matter for the king, inasmuch as no great king or ruler has *ever* asked anything like this of any magician, conjurer or Chaldean. 11 "Moreover, the thing which the king demands is difficult, and there is no one else who could declare it to the king except gods, whose dwelling place is not with *mortal* flesh."

12 Because of this the king became indignant and very furious and gave orders to destroy all the wise men of Babylon. 13 So the decree went forth that the wise men should be slain; and they looked for Daniel and his friends to kill *them*.

14 Then Daniel replied with discretion and discernment to Arioch, the captain of the king's bodyguard, who had gone forth to slay the wise men of Babylon; 15 he said to Arioch, the king's commander, "For what reason is the decree from the king *so* urgent?" Then Arioch informed Daniel about the matter. 16 So Daniel went in and requested of the king that he would give him time, in order that he might declare the interpretation to the king.

17 Then Daniel went to his house and informed his friends, Hananiah, Mishael and Azariah, about the matter, 18 so that they might request compassion from the God of heaven concerning this mystery, so that Daniel and his friends would not be destroyed with the rest of the wise men of Babylon.

The Secret Is Revealed to Daniel

19 Then the mystery was revealed to Daniel in a night vision. Then Daniel blessed the God of heaven; 20 Daniel said, "Let the name of God be blessed forever and ever, For wisdom and power belong to Him.

21 "It is He who changes the times and the epochs; He removes kings and establishes kings; He gives wisdom to wise men And knowledge to men of understanding.

22 "It is He who reveals the profound and hidden things; He knows what is in the darkness, And the light dwells with Him.

23 "To You, O God of my fathers, I give thanks and praise, For You have given me wisdom and power; Even now You have made known to me what we requested of You, For You have made known to us the king's matter."

24 Therefore, Daniel went in to Arioch, whom the king had appointed to destroy the wise men of Babylon; he went and spoke to him as follows: "Do not destroy the wise men of Babylon! Take me into the king's presence, and I will declare the interpretation to the king."

25 Then Arioch hurriedly brought Daniel into the king's presence and spoke to him as follows: "I have found a man among the exiles from Judah who can make the interpretation known to the king!" 26 The king said to Daniel, whose name was Belteshazzar, "Are you able to make known to me the dream which I have seen and its interpretation?" 27 Daniel answered before the king and said, "As for the mystery about which the king has inquired, neither wise men, conjurers, magicians *nor* diviners are able to declare *it* to the king. 28 "However, there is a God in heaven who reveals mysteries, and He has made known to King Nebuchadnezzar what will take place in the latter days. This was your dream and the visions in your mind *while* on your bed. 29 "As for you, O king, *while* on your bed your thoughts turned to what would take place in the future; and He who reveals mysteries has made known to you what will take place. 30 "But as for me, this mystery has not been revealed to me for any wisdom residing in me more than *in* any*other* living man, but for the purpose of making the interpretation known to the king, and that you may understand the thoughts of your mind.

The King's Dream

31 "You, O king, were looking and behold, there was a single great statue; that statue, which was large and of extraordinary splendor, was standing in front of you, and its appearance was awesome. 32 "The head of that statue *was made* of fine gold, its breast and its arms of silver, its belly and its thighs of bronze, 33 its legs of iron, its feet partly of iron and partly of clay. 34 "You continued looking until a stone was cut out without hands, and it struck the statue on its feet of iron and clay and crushed them. 35 "Then the iron, the clay, the bronze, the silver and the gold were crushed all at the same time and became like chaff from the summer threshing floors; and the wind carried them away so that not a trace of them was found. But the stone that struck the statue became a great mountain and filled the whole earth.

The Interpretation—Babylon the First Kingdom

36 "This *was* the dream; now we will tell its interpretation before the king. 37 "You, O king, are the king of kings, to whom the God of heaven has given the kingdom, the power, the strength and the glory; 38 and wherever the sons of men dwell, *or* the beasts of the field, or the birds of the sky, He has given *them* into your hand and has caused you to rule over them all. You are the head of gold.

The Matrix: Summary

At the beginning of the film we listen to a conversation between two members of Morpheus' crew, Trinity and Cypher.

Trinity suspects their dialogue is overheard by the agents and intends to leave. Police officers run into her location, room N° 303 in a hotel called "Heart O' The City" and want to arrest Trinity who easily defeats the six policemen.

Outside the hotel three agents appear dressed in black suits – Agent Smith, Agent Jones and Agent Brown. Trinity brings it off to escape from them but the agents are satisfied having proved the loyality of their informator and start a search for Neo

The underground hacker Morpehus stamped in the matrix as a dangerous criminal intrigues Neo who is searching for him already for a long time.

Trinity cracks Thomas' personal computer and writes him that he were observed and the Matrix had him. Trinity tells Neo to follow the white rabbit.

At this moment the door bell rings – Neo's friend Choix has come for a CD which Neo retains in the book "Simulacra and Simulation" by Jean Baudrillard.

When Choix receives the CD he says: Hallelujah. You're my saviour, man. My own personal Jesus Christ." Neo warns him of the risk of being caught using the illgal CD and Choix replies:

"Yeah, I know. This never happened, you don't exist."

Choix proposes Neo to go with him and his friends to a night club. Firstly, Neo refuses but than he notices a tattoo on the shoulder of the girlfriend of Choix, Dujour. This is a white rabbit. So Neo follows Choix and Dujour and meets Trinity in the club.

Neo already knows Trinity as a hacker who has cracked the IRS D-base.

She warns him of danger: "They're watching you, Neo." and seems to know quite much about the life of Thomas Anderson and reveals that. The audience gets to know that Thomas Anderson hardly sleeps at night and searches for Morpheus to find the answer on the question "What is the Matrix?".

In the next scene Neo wakes up late in the morning and goes to the software company he works for. After having an unpleasant conversation with his boss concerning the delay Neo receives a parcel with a cellular phone in it. As soon as he picks it up, it rings. Morpheus is on the phone telling Neo that he has to escape for the agents are coming for him. The only way to escape is to get to the roof using the scafford. Neo doesn't muster up enough courage and leaves the building in the custody of the agents.

In an interrogation room the agents confront Neo. They have a dossier on him and know that Neo lives a dual existence. They oppress Neo and make him an offer. Neo should help them to catch the dangerous criminal Morpheus in exchange for amnesty. Neo impolitely refuses and demands an phone call he had a right on. Agent Smith asks Neo how a phone call could help is Neo is unable to speak and tha latter finds his lips litterary sealed. Thereupon the agents implunt a shrimp-like bug in Neo's stomach through the belly-button.

The next scene shows Neo who wakes up in the morning assuming he has dreamt everything. At that time his phone rings, Morpheus is on the line telling Neo he would be picked up on the Adams Street .

Neo goes there and sees Trinity and two further members of the crew, Switch and Apoc. After having removed the probe of Neo's stomach, Trinity takes Neo to Morpheus.

The latter explains that he has been searching for Neo his entire life and asks if Neo feels like Alice in Wonderland, falling down the rabbit hole.

Morpheus tells Neo that they exist in the Matrix, a false reality their minds are caught in to hide the truth.

The truth is that everyone in the world is a slave, "born into bondage, born into a prison […]. A prison for your mind".

Morpheus holds out a blue and a red pill. He says if Neo takes tha blue one he will wake up and "believe whatever you want to believe." But if he takes the red pill, then "you stay in Wonderland and I show you how deep the rabbit hole goes." Neo takes the red pill and follows Morpheus through double doors into a room with computer terminals and other machines.

Neo is asked to take a seat and connected to the computer.

He is told that pill he took is part of a trace program, to "disrupt his input/output carrier signal" so that they can pinpoint him. When Neo lookes at a crushed mirror next to him it reforms itself. Morpheus asks Neo: "Have you ever had a dream, Neo, that you were so sure was real? What if you were unable to wake from that dream? How would you know the difference, between the dream world...and the real world....?" Neo curiously touches the mirror, the silver takes Neo over and he blacks out.

Neo, hairless and nacked, awakens inside a purple embryonic pod pulling out from a circular building Thick black tubes are plugged into the back of his skull, his spine and he rest of his body. Around him are thousands of such pods, all containing bodies.

A robot grabs Neo, the tubes detach and Neo is flushed down a tube into a pond.
He looks up to a square of light, is picked up and finds himself surrounded by Morpheus's crew again. Before they have been dressed in leather and latex but now they wear simple knit robes. Morpheus says to Neo "Welcome to the real world." And the latter blacks out.
Neo drifts in and out of consciousness. At one point he asks, "Am I dead?" "Far from it," replies Morpheus. When he awakens again, wearing nothing but a linen sheet, many needles are put inside his body. "Why do my eyes hurt?" he asks. "You have never used them," Morpheus replies.

Neo finally awakes "What is this place?" Neo asks. "The more important question is when," says Morpheus, "You believe it is the year 1999. When in fact it is closer to the year 2199." Morpheus continues to say that they really don't know when it is. He proceeds to give Neo a tour of his ship, the Nebuchadnezzar (they pass a plaque stating it was built in 2069). Neo is introduced to Morpheus's crew including Trinity, Apoc, Switch, Cypher, Tank, Dozer and Mouse.
Neo is than connected to the computer and awakes in a world of all white. He is in the Construct, a programm preparing the rebel to dealing with the Matrix.
Morpheus shows Neo images of two different worlds – the false reality Neo is used to live in and the dark and menacing real world how It looks like after the War between humans and machines.
Neo rejects this information and pulls himself out of the Construct feeling physically sick. When he awakes again he asks Morpheus if he can go back. "No, but if you could, would you really want to?", - Morpheus replies.
He explains to Neo the origins of the resistance. When the Matrix had been first built, a man had been born inside it who had been able to change everything in the programm. This man had taught some other humans the truth about their slavery within the Matrix. After his death the Oracle had prophesied his return. Morpheus believes, he has found the saviour and this is Neo. According to the Oracle the return of the One would mean the destruction of the Matrix.

On the next day Neo starts his training and learns at first martial art. Afterwards he fights with Morpheus and learns that the rules within the Matrix can be bent or broken because it is just a computer program. Then a jump program is loaded and Neo should jump from one skyscraper on another like Morpheus who tells him to free his mind and realise that this is not real. Neo falls on the ground and has blood in his mouth when returned in the real world. He wants to know if one dies in the reality having died in the Matrix. Morpheus tells Neo that it is his mind which makes the death real.

"The body cannot live without the mind," says Morpheus underlining the very real danger faced in the simulation.

After that Morpheus and Neo are walking down the city in a simulation program and Morpheus explains that as long the humans are in the Matrix they are their enemies and can transform into agents. Agents are sentient programs that "can move in and out of any software hard-wired into their system, meaning that they can take over anyone in the Matrix program." Thus Morpheus and his crew survive the Agents by running from them. No one before could fight against them but the agents also live in the world of rules and their speed and force have their limits.

Morpheus and Neo have to return on Nebukadnezzar after Cypher's call.

A squiddy, a search and destroy sentinel pursues the ship. The crew sets the ship down in a huge sewer system and turn off the power so that the sentinels can't detect them.

At night Neo comes to Cypher who is working at a computer streaming with green code. Cypher offers Neo a drink and tells him that he knows what Neo is now thinking, he is regretting having taken the red pill. Neo does not replie.

In the following scene we see Cypher and agent Smith in a restaurant. Cypher enjoys the meal and tells Smith that after nine years in the reality he has discovered that "ignorance is bliss." He wants to be reinserted into the Matrix and has thus betrayed his crew and helps Smith to catch Morpheus, the commander of the ship. Morpheus is the only one who knows the access codes to the mainframe in Zion, the last human city located near the earth's core. If Smith gets the codes Zion wil be destroyed and the humans will be ultimately defeated.

On the next day everyone of the crew except Tank and Dozer drive to the Oracle.

The Oracle, Morpheus explains, has been with them since the beginning of the Resistance. She is the one who made the Prophecy of the One and that Morpheus would be the one to find him. She can help Neo find the path, he says.

Inside the apartment of the Oracle are other potentials: a mother figure and numerous children. One child levitates blocks, one reads Asian literature, another is playing chess. Neo's attention is captures by a little boy bending spoons. The boy gives one spoon to Neo and says, "Do not try and bend the spoon, that's impossible. Instead, only try to realize the truth...that there is no spoon." Neo bends the spoon as he's called in to see the Oracle.

The Oracle sizes Neo up reminding one on a medicinal investigation and asks Neo what does he think about Morpheus' convincement.

Neo says he does not know and the Oracle does not enlighten him but she reveals to Neo that Morpheus' belief is that strong that he will sacrifice his own life to save Neo.

As the crew returns to their jack point, Neo, walking up the stairs, Neo notices a black cat appearing twice. "Deja vu," he says. The others are worried because a déjà vu can appear when the computer parameters are reset. Outside, the phone line is cut.

Mouse is killed by the police and location of the rest of the crew is detected. As agent Smith comes in, Morpheus springs at him telling Trinity to bring Neo out of the building.

Cypher returns to the reality earlier than the others, kills Dozer and wounds Tank intending to unplug the crew members while speaking to Trinity on the telephone: "He lied to us, Trinity. He tricked us. If you'd have told

us the truth, we woulda told you to shove that red pill

right up your ass!

Trinity : That's not true Cypher, he set us free."

Firstly Cypher unplugs Switch and Apoc and they die in the Matrix. Then he wants to unplug Neo and says: " If Neo's The One, then there'd have to be some kinda miracle to stop me." Suddenly Tank, who Cypher thought to be dead, shoots the betrayer and helps Trinity and Neo to get out the Matrix.

Meanwhile Morpheus is in the office on the top floor of a skyscraper, with three agents. He is handcuffed to the chair he's sitting on and is pumped full of serum. He is hooked up to various monitors with white disk electrodes.

Agent Smith tells Morpheus that the first version of the Matrix was designed as a utopia, engineered to make everyone happy but people did not want to accept the program and "entire crops were lost" (Smith means people the machines are growing in the cocoons). Smith explains that some of the machines have thought they would not know the programming language to create the perfect human world. But Smith is convinced that "as a species, human beings define their reality through misery and suffering. The perfect world was a dream that your primitive cerebrum kept trying to wake up from."

That is why the programm was redesigned.

On Nebukadnezzar Tank says that the only solution is to unplug Morpheus, otherwise the machines would get the codes to the mainframes of Zion's computer and the humans would be wiped out.

Neo stops himand reveals the prophecy to Tank and Trinity. He wants to enter the Matrix and resque Morpheus ready to sacrifice his own life if necessary.

Meanwhile Agent Smith continues to soloquise about human race.

He compares the humans to a virus because we spread in an area as long as all ressources are consumed, and we have to spread to a new area.

As Morpheus's mind is not yet broken into, Smith commands the other agents to leave them alone and removes his earphone.

He admits that he hates the Matrix, "this zoo, this prison." He needs the codes to Zion for without Zion there is no need in Smith within the Matrix.

Meanwhile Trinity and Neo have entered the building heavily armed. They kill the guards and enter an elevator.

In the elevator, Trinity arms a bomb. They both climb to the elevator roof and Neo severs the cable after having said "There is no spoon". Against the gravity, Neo transport them upwards and the elevetor falls down exploding.

One of the agents is sent to kill the rebels but Neo fights with him what nobody of the humans has done before. He moves almost as fast as the machine.

After having defeated the agent, they take a helicopter and bring Morpheus out from the building. The helicopter's hydraulic line is shut by one of the agents. Trinity, who pilots it, is in danger. Neo saves her showing incredible power.

On the ship Tank says: "I knew it; he's the One."

"Do you believe it now, Trinity?" asks Morpheus as he approaches the two. Neo tries to tell him that the Oracle told him the opposite but Morpheus says, "She told you exactly what you needed to hear." They call Tank, who tells them of an exit in a subway near them.

After Morpheus and Trinity exit the Matrix, Smith appears, having appropriated the body of a homeless lying in the subway, and shatters the ear piece of the phone; it' is impossible for Neo to exit there now.

Instead of running away Neo fights with Smith and defeats him.

Smith appropriates another body and follows Neo who heads for the stares.

Meanwhile the Sentinels have arrived to attack the Nebuchadnezzar, the crew waits for Neo and can't charge the electromagnetic pulse to remain undiscovered.

Neo calls Tank who gives him a direction.

At this moment the Sentinels begin to tear the ship apart. Neo arrives at the "Heart O' the City Hotel." Closely followed by the agents. Tank tells him to go to room 303.

Meanwhile the Sentinels are inside of the ship.

Having reached the room Neo is shut by Smith and physically dies, he has no pulse.

On the ship Trinity speaks to Neo confessing her love and begging him to stand up. Neo resurrects and is now able to see the codes of the Matrix which makes it easy for him to defeat Smith.

The other agents run away. Neo exits the Matrix and kisses Trinity.

In the following scene we hear Neo's voice: "I know you're out there. I can feel you now. I know that you're afraid... you're afraid of us. You're afraid of change. I don't know the future. I didn't come here to tell you how this is going to end. I came here to tell you how it's going to begin. I'm going to hang up this phone, and then I'm going to show these people what you don't want them to see. I'm going to show them a world without you. A world without rules and controls, without borders or boundaries. A world where anything is possible. Where we go from there is a choice I leave to you."

in the Matrix world Neo hangs up the phone and takes a flight.

References

Books

[AHD:00] The American Heritage Dictionary of the English Language. Houghton Mifflin Harcourt, 2000

[Bab:10.1] The History of Computer Science

[Bab:10.2] The History of Artificial Intelligence: Artificial Neural Networks and Expert Systems*

[Bab:10.3] The Matrix: Summary*

[Bau:94] Simulacra and Simulation. Jean Baudrillard. University of Michigan Press, 1994

[Bla:99] Lexikon der buddhistischen Symbole.Schirner Verlag, Darmstadt, 1999

[Cam:03] Cambridge Advanced Learner's Dictionary. Cambridge University Press, New York, 2003

[Des:99] Discourse on Method and Meditations on First Philosophy. R. Descartes.

[Haw:98] A Brief History of Time. Bantam Dell, 1998

[Hem:95] Leben aus der Einheit. Klaus Hemmerle. Herder Verlag, Freiburg, 1995

[Gus:00] Wahrnehmung. Eine Einführung in die Psychologie der menschlichen Informationsaufnahme. Rainer Guski. Kohlhammer Urban, 2000

Translated by D. Cress. Hackett Publishing Company, 1999.

[Kan:03] Critique of Pure Reason. Immanuel Kant. Dover Publications, 2003.

[Kan:74] Kritik der Urteilskraft. Felix Meiner Verlag, 1974

[Kan:85] Kritik der praktischen Vernunft. Felix Meiner Verlag, 1985

[Mon:06] Nietzsche-Studien. Mazzino Montinari. De Gruyter, 2006

[NAB:95] New American Standard Bible. The Lockman Foundation,1995

[ORg:08] A brief History of Computing . Gerard O'Regan. Springer Verlag, London, 2008*

[Pen:89] The Emperor's New Mind. Roger Penrose. Oxford University Press, 1989

[Pen:96] Shadows of the Mind: A Search for the Missing Science of Consciousness. Roger Penrose. Oxford University Press, New York, 1996

[See:03] Die Matrix entschlüsselt. Georg Seesslen. Bertz Verlag, Berlin, 2003

[The:06] The Oxford Thesaurus of English. Oxford University Press, New York, 2006

Internet sources [Status 05.03.2010]

1.   Ancient Greek Mathematics. Kidipede. Portland State University.
http://www.historyforkids.org/learn/greeks/science/math/

2.   Ancient Egyptian Number Hieroglyphs. Egyptian Math. Eyelid Productions.
http://www.eyelid.co.uk/numbers.htm

3.   An overview of Babylonian mathematics. School of Mathematical and Computational
Sciences. University of St Andrews.
http://www-groups.dcs.st-and.ac.uk/~history/HistTopics/Babylonian_mathematics.html

4.   An overview of Indian mathematics. School of Mathematical and Computational
Sciences. University of St Andrews.
http://www-groups.dcs.st-and.ac.uk/~history/HistTopics/Indian_mathematics.html

5.   About Pascaline. School of Mathematical and Computer Sciences (MACS). Heriot-Watt
University.
http://www.macs.hw.ac.uk/~greg/calculators/pascal/About_Pascaline.htm

6.   Blaise Pascal (1623-1662). About.com: Inventors. The New York Times Company.
http://inventors.about.com/library/inventors/blpascal.htm

7.   http://pkirs.utep.edu/mit5312/Additional%20Coverage/Tutorials/ISTypes/Early/leibniz_w
heel.htm

8.   History of the Jacquard automated loom. Suspenders.com.
http://www.suspenders.com/jacquard-history.htm

9.   The Babbage Engine: A Brief History. Computer History Museum.
http://www.computerhistory.org/babbage/history/

10.   The Babbage Engine: A Modern Sequel. Computer History Museum.
http://www.computerhistory.org/babbage/modernsequel/

11.   The Babbage Engine: The Engines. Computer History Museum.
http://www.computerhistory.org/babbage/engines/

12.   The Babbage Engine: Overview. Computer History Museum.
http://www.computerhistory.org/babbage/overview/

13.   Herman Hollerith: The World's First Statistical Engineer. Mark Russo. University of
Rochester.
http://www.history.rochester.edu/steam/hollerith/

14.   Herman Hollerith. Computing History. Columbia University.
http://www.columbia.edu/acis/history/hollerith.html

15.   From the U.S. Constitution to IBM. Wittenberg University.
http://www4.wittenberg.edu/academics/mathcomp/bjsdir/history0.shtml

16.   The IBM Automatic Sequence Controlled Calculator. Computing History. Columbia University.
http://www.columbia.edu/acis/history/mark1.html

17.   ENIAC. IEEE Virtual Museum.
http://www.ieee-virtual-museum.org/collection/event.php?id=3456881&lid=1

18.   Programming the ENIAC. Computer History. Columbia University.
http://www.columbia.edu/acis/history/eniac.html

19.   Part 3: Konrad Zuse's First Computer -- The Z1. EPE.
http://www.epemag.com/zuse/part3a.htm

20.   John Louis von Neumann. CS Dept. Virginia Tech/Norfolk State University.
http://ei.cs.vt.edu/~history/VonNeumann.html

21.   The First Stored Program Computer -- EDVAC. Maxfield & Montrose Interactive Inc.
http://www.maxmon.com/1946ad.htm

22.   The Univac was the First Commercial Computer Circa 1950. Associated Content, Inc.
http://www.associatedcontent.com/article/380960/the_univac_was_the_first_commercial.html

23.   The IBM 701 Defense Calculator. Computing History. Columbia University.
http://www.columbia.edu/acis/history/701.html

24.   First-Generation Computers. The Development of Computers. Hagar.
http://hagar.up.ac.za/catts/learner/andria/5FirstGenComp.html

25.   The Invention of the Transistor. Following the Path of Discovery. Julian Rubin.
http://www.juliantrubin.com/bigten/transistorexperiments.html

26.   The FORTRAN Programming Language. College of Engineering & Computer Science. University of Michigan.
http://www.engin.umd.umich.edu/CIS/course.des/cis400/fortran/fortran.html

27.   The COBOL Programming Language. College of Engineering & Computer Science. The University of Michigan - Dearborn.
http://www.engin.umd.umich.edu/CIS/course.des/cis400/cobol/cobol.html

28.   1960: DEC PDP-1 Precursor to the Minicomputer. CED in the History of Media Technology.
http://www.cedmagic.com/history/dec-pdp-1.html

29. Altair BASIC programming language. Knowledgerush.com.

http://www.knowledgerush.com/kr/encyclopedia/Altair_BASIC_programming_language/

30. CRAY 1. The History of Computing Project.

http://www.thocp.net/hardware/cray_1.htm

31. Computer Science Reaches Historic Breakthrough. IBM.com.

http://www.ibm.com/ibm/ideasfromibm/us/roadrunner/20080609/index.shtml

32. The Apple Store. Apple Inc.

http://store.apple.com/us

33. The Unusual History of Microsoft Windows. About.com: Inventors.

http://inventors.about.com/od/mstartinventions/a/Windows.htm

34. Mac OS X 10.0. Ars Technica, LLC.

http://arstechnica.com/reviews/01q2/macos-x-final/macos-x-1.html

35. ARPANET -- The First Internet. livinginternet.

http://www.livinginternet.com/i/ii_arpanet.htm

36. Number Symbolism

http://www.khandro.net/about_numbers.htm

37. Digital Computer – Britannica Online Encyclopedia

http://www.britannica.com/EBchecked/topic/163278/digital-computer

38. Professor Cyborg – If we want to stop machines from taking over, we better start becoming more like them

http://www.salon.com/tech/feature/1999/10/20/cyborg/

39. Matrix Secrets explained

http://www.matrix-explained.com/

40. Symbolism of Esoteric Numbers

http://www.numerologiafuturo.com/symbolism_esoteric.php

41. Pythagoras – Early Concepts of Number and Number Mysticism

http://www.mathgym.com.au/history/pythagoras/pythnum.htm

42. Computer Systems

http://cnx.org/content/m27733/latest/

43. Von-Neumann-Architecture

http://tams-www.informatik.uni-hamburg.de/applets/baukasten/DA/VNR_Einleitung.html

44. Analogue Computer – The Columbia Electronic Encyclopedia

www.cc.columbia.edu/cu/cup/

45. Analogue and Digital Computing
http://www.bookrags.com/research/analog-vs-digital-computing-wcs/

46. From the U.S. Constitution to IBM
http://www4.wittenberg.edu/academics/mathcomp/bjsdir/history0.shtml

47. Higher-Order Theories of Consciousness
http://plato.stanford.edu/entries/consciousness-higher/

48. Modus Ponens and Modus Tollens – the Britannica Online Encyclopedia
http://www.britannica.com/EBchecked/topic/387439/modus-ponens

49. Spiritual Symbolism in The Matrix
http://www.voidspace.org.uk/cyberpunk/matrix_spirit.shtml

50. Gedächtnis: Kognitive Neurowissenschaften
http://www.neurowissenschaft.ch/oldNeuro/Lehre/WS0607/Kog1_VL/KogNeu-Gedaechtnis-reduced2.pdf

51. Smallest Computer in the World
http://www.youtube.com/watch?v=iaz63L8x0Z8

52. Cipher Etymology, Origin and History
http://www.wordnik.com/words/cipher/etymologies

53. A Definition of Dystopia
http://hem.passagen.se/replikant/dystopia_definition.htm

54. Sensient machines
http://elib.uni-stuttgart.de/opus/volltexte/2007/3213/pdf/Ue_149_Kobrinskij.pdf

55. Information on Morphine
http://www.drugs.com/morphine.html

56. Babylonian God Nabu
http://www.absoluteastronomy.com/topics/Nabu

57. The Matrix Script
http://dc-mrg.english.ucsb.edu/WarnerTeach/E192/matrix/Matrix.script.html

58. About "The Matrix"
http://www.imdb.de/title/tt0133093/

59. Morpheus, God of Dreams
http://www.theoi.com/Daimon/OneirosMorpheus.html

60. About "The Matrix"
http://www.imdb.de/title/tt0133093/

Film sources

1. The Matrix. Written and directed by Larry and Andy Wachowski. Warner Bros. Pictures, 1999
2. The Animatrix. Directed by Larry and Andy Wachowski. Warner Bros. Home Video, 2003